dog names

dog names

Jenny Linford

RYLAND
PETERS
& SMALL

LONDON NEW YORK

Designer Iona Hoyle
Senior Editor Miriam Hyslop
Picture Researcher Emily Westlake
Production Gordana Simakovic
Art Director Anne-Marie Bulat
Publishing Director Alison Starling

First published in the United Kingdom in 2006
by Ryland Peters & Small
20–21 Jockey's Fields
London WC1R 4BW
www.rylandpeters.com

10 9 8 7 6 5 4 3 2 1

ISBN-10: 1-84597-271-6
ISBN-13: 978-1-84597-271-4

A CIP record for this book is available from the
British Library.

Printed and bound in China

contents

introduction

Bringing home a small puppy is one of life's great pleasures. Owning a new puppy, however, does bring with it a particular dilemma. What should this endearing little creature be called? It's so important to find a name that you really like (bearing in mind that you will have to call to your dog in public!) and which suits your new canine companion. While, of course, classic names like Dog or Scruff continue to be popular, there is a rich seam of possible dog names to mine. Choose from names that reflect your dog's colouring and markings, like Jet, Spot or Whisky, or its personality, so Caesar for commanding dogs or Frisky for lively canines. Alternatively, name your puppy after famous fictional or real-life canines such as Lassie or Tintin's Snowy. With over 1,000 names to choose from, naming your new puppy has never been so easy or so much fun.

classic dogs

Angus
An old-fashioned name for male dogs.

Animal
A fundamental name for dogs.

Atom
For small, fast-moving dogs of either sex.

Bach
A music-inspired, punning name for vocal dogs.

Bali
A tropical name for mellow dogs of either sex.

Baloo
For large, friendly dogs, after the bear in *The Jungle Book*.

Banana
A fruit-inspired name for dogs.

Banjo
A music-inspired name for vocal dogs.

Barker
For noisy male dogs.

Baskerville
For huge hounds, after Sir Arthur Conan Doyle's creation *The Hound of the Baskervilles*.

Beachcomber
For male dogs who enjoy finding things.

Bear
For large, bear-like dogs.

Beau
For attractive dogs; from the French for 'handsome'.

Big
A simple name for large dogs.

Bingo
For lucky dogs; after the game.

Blade
For sleek dogs of either sex.

Blue
A popular name for dogs of either sex and any colour.

Bolero
A musical name for vocal dogs.

Bonkers
An affectionate name for mad dogs.

Bono
For bone-loving canines.

Bonzo
A classic male dog name.

Boo
For surprising dogs of either sex.

classic dogs

9

Boomerang
For dogs that are good at
returning to their owners.

Booster
For energetic male dogs.

Boots
For dogs with distinctive-
coloured paws.

Bouncer
A simple name for lively dogs.

Bow
An endearing name for canines.

Bubbles
For cheerful, light-hearted dogs
of either sex.

Buddy
A classic name for friendly
male dogs.

Bug
A cheery, insect-inspired name
for dogs of either sex.

Bumble
An affectionate name for slow-
moving dogs.

Burger
A food-inspired name for
greedy dogs.

Buster
A classic name for friendly
male dogs.

Butch
Traditional name for tough dogs.

Butterball
An affectionate name for chubby
dogs of either sex.

Buttons
For bright-eyed dogs.

Buzz
For speedy dogs of either sex.

Capricorn
A Zodiac-inspired name for
nimble-footed dogs.

Cello
A music-inspired name for
vocal dogs.

Challenger
For male dogs who enjoy
a challenge.

Chewbacca
A *Star Wars*-inspired name for
large, hairy dogs.

Chewy
For dogs who can't resist getting
their teeth into things.

Chianti
A wine-inspired name for dogs
of either sex.

Chip
A down-to-earth name for
food-loving dogs.

Chowder
A food-inspired name for
greedy dogs.

Chum
A traditional name for friendly
male dogs.

Chutney
A relish-inspired name for dogs
of either sex.

Clown
For dogs with a sense of humour.

Comet
An astrological name for dogs
of either sex.

Couscous
For greedy dogs of either sex;
after the North African staple.

Coyote
After the wild wolf.

Cracker
A cheerful, food-inspired name
for dogs of either sex.

Cranberry
A fruit-inspired name for dogs
of either sex.

Crash
For clumsy male dogs.

Crumpet
A humorous, food-inspired
name for greedy dogs.

Cruncher
For dogs who enjoy chewing bones.

Crusher
For strong, tough male dogs.

Dandy
For elegant male dogs.

Dart
For fast-moving dogs of either sex.

Dash
For dogs that like to run around.

Dawn
For early-rising female dogs.

Delicious
For food-loving dogs of either sex.

Digger
For dogs who can't resist a bit of digging.

Dingo
After the Australian wild dog.

Dino
For large dogs; abbreviated from 'dinosaur'.

Dog
A fundamental canine name.

Doggle
An affectionate name for lively dogs of either sex.

Doodle
An endearing name for dogs of either sex.

Doughnut
A cheery name for greedy dogs.

Dumbo
For large grey dogs, after Disney's loveable elephant.

Dumpling
An affectionate name for rotund dogs.

Dynamite
For explosive male dogs.

Elvis
A rock 'n' roll name for music-loving hound dogs.

E.T.
An extra-terrestrial name for lovable dogs.

Fang
For sharp-toothed dogs.

Fatso
A humorous name for portly dogs.

Fetch
A classic dog name for dogs that enjoy retrieving sticks for their owners.

Fidget
For small, restless dogs.

Fido
A classic male dog name.

Flapjack
A food-inspired name for greedy male dogs.

Flea
An affectionate name for small dogs.

Flipflop
For mellow dogs of either sex.

classic dogs

11

Football
For dogs who love to play with balls.

Frisbee
A game-inspired name.

Fungus
A food-inspired name for dogs of either sex.

Galaxy
An apt name for large dogs.

Gale
For dogs who enjoy wild weather.

Garlic
A food-inspired name for dogs.

Genie
For dogs of either sex.

Gobble
For greedy dogs of either sex.

Goliath
For large, male dogs.

Gremlin
For dogs that cause all sorts of trouble.

Growler
For intimidating, male guard dogs.

Gucci
For fashionable dogs of either sex; after the Italian fashion house.

Gulper
For greedy male dogs.

Gumdrop
A humorous name for dogs of either sex.

Gypsy
For wandering canines.

Heinz
For mongrels, after Heinz's '57 Varieties'.

Helix
A DNA-inspired name for dogs of either sex.

Hobbit
A *The Lord of the Rings*-inspired name for small furry dogs.

Horse
A popular name for large, strong dogs.

Hot Dog
A food-inspired name for greedy dogs.

Howl
For dogs who enjoy howling at the moon (or the postman).

Hunter
A classic name for good hunting dogs.

Hurricane
For enthusiastic, energetic

canines that leave a trail of destruction in their path.

Jabberwocky
A humorous name, from Lewis Carroll's poem.

Jambalaya
A food-inspired name for greedy dogs.

Jaws
For large-mouthed, sharp-toothed dogs.

Jelly
A humorous name for nervous dogs of either sex.

Jellybean
An endearing name for loveable, sweet-natured canines of either sex.

Jimbob
A humorous name for male dogs, after the character in TV series *The Waltons*.

Jitterbug
A dance-inspired name for dogs of either sex.

K-9
A punning, robotic name for canines.

Ki
A classic French name, from the Breton for 'dog'.

Killer
A classic name for savage, feral dogs of either sex.

King
A popular name for regal male canines.

Lamb
For sweet-tempered, gentle dogs of either sex.

Leviathan
A biblical name for large, imposing dogs.

London
A capital name for city-living dogs.

Lucky
An affectionate name for dogs of either sex.

Macintosh
For dogs who enjoy getting wet; after the waterproof raincoat.

Magic
A name for dogs of either sex.

Meatball
For large dogs with a healthy appetite.

Meatloaf
A food-inspired name for greedy male dogs.

Mighty
For big, strong male dogs.

Milkshake
A drink-inspired name for thirsty dogs of either sex.

Mini
For small female dogs.

Miss
A classic name for female dogs.

Mister
A classic name for male dogs.

Misto
From the Italian for 'mixed'; ideal for mongrels.

Molecule
For small dogs of either sex.

Mopsy
For small, very hairy dogs of either sex.

Muddles
An affectionate name for confused dogs.

Muddy
A self-explanatory name for dogs who enjoy getting dirty.

Mungo
A classic name for male dogs.

Mutt
A down-to-earth name for dogs.

Nantucket
For dogs who enjoy having a whale of a time; after the American island with a history of whaling.

Navigator
For dogs who are good at finding the way.

Nemo
For water-loving male dogs; after Jules Verne's literary creation Captain Nemo.

Neutron
A molecule-inspired name for small dogs of either sex.

Nibbler
For dogs of either sex who just can't resist a nibble.

Nipper
For male dogs with a tendency to nip.

Nippy
For quick and nimble dogs of either sex.

Nomad
For wandering dogs of either sex.

Nutmeg
A spice-inspired name for dogs of either sex.

Parma
A food-inspired name – after Italian Parma ham – for dogs who enjoy fine food.

Paws
A classic dog's name.

Pesto
A food-inspired name for dogs of either sex.

Pickles
For naughty canines that often find themselves in trouble.

Piglet
An affectionate name for small, greedy dogs of either sex.

Pirate
For cheeky male dogs with a tendency to steal things.

Pixie
For small, enchanting dogs of either sex.

Podge
A humorous name for chubby dogs of either sex.

Pudding
A food-inspired name for sweet dogs of either sex.

Pup
A traditional name for youthful canines.

Quince
A fruit-inspired name for dogs of either sex.

Racer
For fast-moving dogs.

Radar
For dogs who are good at finding their way.

Rags
An old-fashioned dog name.

Ragu
A food-inspired name for greedy male dogs.

Rambler
For dogs who enjoy long, leisurely strolls.

Ranger
For outdoor-loving dogs.

Ravioli
A pasta-inspired name for food-loving dogs.

Regalo
From the Italian for 'present', for dogs who are gifts.

Ricochet
For speedy, all-over-the-place hounds.

Rocket
For fast-moving male dogs.

Roly-Poly
A cheerful, affectionate name for chubby dogs.

Roma
A cosmopolitan name for city dogs; after the Italian capital.

Roo
A marsupial-inspired name for high-jumping dogs.

Rover
For dogs who like to explore.

Ruff
A classic name for male dogs.

Rugrat
Inspired by the children's cartoon series.

Runt
For small dogs, or the runt of the litter.

Safari
For adventurous dogs who enjoy long journeys.

Salsa
A dance-inspired name for rhythmic dogs of either sex.

Sandwich
A fun, food-inspired name for greedy dogs.

Sausage
An affectionate name for small dogs.

Scallywag
For cheeky male dogs.

Scrabble
A game-inspired name for dogs of either sex.

Scrap
For small, scruffy dogs.

Scruff
For endearingly messy dogs.

Sesame
A food-inspired name for dogs of either sex.

Shadow
For dogs of either sex who like to follow their owner.

Shaggy
An affectionate name for hairy dogs.

Shrimp
An endearing name for small dogs of either sex.

Sirius
For male dogs, after Sirius the dog star.

Skip
A cheerful, monosyllabic name.

Sky
For graceful dogs, especially blue-grey ones.

Slipper
For dogs with a taste for footwear.

Smiffy
An endearing name.

Smudge
For messy dogs of either sex.

Snappy
For bad-tempered dogs.

Sniff
For dogs who like sniffing about.

Snuff
A humorous name for male canines.

Snufkin
An endearing name for male dogs; from *The Moomins*.

Snuffles
For dogs who enjoy sniffing.

Socks
For dogs with distinctive markings on their paws.

Sparky
For bright, lively dogs.

Spike
A classic dog name.

Spitfire
For speedy dogs.

Sprocket
A humorous name for male dogs.

Sputnik
A space-inspired name for male dogs; after the world's first artificial satellite.

Squeak
For small-voiced dogs of either sex.

Star
For bright-eyed, night-loving dogs of either sex.

Strider
For long-legged dogs who enjoy going for walks.

Sumo
For large dogs; after the Japanese wrestlers.

Superdog
For wonder-dogs that always save the day.

Talisman
For lucky dogs of either sex.

Terminator
For formidable male dogs.

Thimble
A classic name for small dogs.

Thor
For loud-barking dogs; after the Norse god of thunder.

Titch
An affectionate name for small dogs.

Toggles
A humorous name for dogs of either sex.

Truffle
A food-inspired name for gourmet male dogs.

Tucker
For greedy dogs of either sex.

Uncle
A family-inspired name.

Waddle
A humorous name for slow-moving dogs.

Waffle
A food-inspired name for greedy dogs of either sex.

Walrus
An expressive name for large, heavy dogs.

Wookiee
A *Star Wars*-inspired name for large, hairy dogs.

Wriggle
A humorous name for fidgety, wriggly dogs.

Yap
For dogs that bark a lot.

Yoga
For mellow, deep-breathing dogs of either sex.

Yogi
For bear-like dogs, after cartoon character Yogi Bear.

Zen
For philosophic dogs.

Zigzag
For dogs that run all over the place.

Zippy
For speedy dogs of either sex.

Zoom
For fast-running dogs.

pedigree dogs

Alaska
For thick-furred, snow-loving dogs, such as Huskies.

Ali
For Boxers, after champion boxer Muhammad Ali.

Aztec
A Mexican-inspired name for Chihuahuas.

Babushka
A female name for Russian dogs, such as Borzoi.

Balzac
A literary name for Poodles; after the French novelist.

Bernard
A classic name for St Bernards.

Blaze
A good name for Red Setters.

Blizzard
A suitable name for snow-loving dogs such as St Bernards, Alaskan Malamute or Siberian Huskies.

Bluebird
For speedy dogs such as Greyhounds and Whippets; after the racing car.

Boatswain
For Newfoundland dogs, after Lord Byron's beloved Newfoundland Boatswain.

Bodger
For Bull Terriers, after the old, tough dog in Sheila Burnford's *The Incredible Journey*.

Bonbon
For sweet-tempered Poodles, from the French for 'sweet'.

Boris
An aristocratic name for Borzois.

Brenin
For regal male Welsh Terriers, from the Welsh for 'king'.

Brunhilde
A Wagnerian name for female German Shepherds.

Burgundy
A wine-inspired name for Red Setters.

Cameron
A traditional name for Scottish Terriers.

Campbell
For speedy dogs such as Whippets or Greyhounds; after racing driver Donald Campbell.

Cari
An affectionate name for female Welsh Terriers, from the Welsh for 'love'.

Cassius
For Boxers, after acclaimed boxer Cassius Clay.

Cheetah
For speedy dogs, such as Greyhounds or Whippets.

Chekhov
A literary name for Russian breeds such as Salukis.

China
For breeds such as Pekingese and Chinese Foos.

Chiquita
A Mexican name for female Chihuahuas.

Churchill
After Britain's Prime Minister Winston Churchill, noted for his bulldog spirit.

Claret
A wine-inspired name for Red Setters.

Clyde
A classic name for Scottish Terriers.

Coco
An elegant French name, particularly apt for Poodles.

Colette
For female Pugs; after the French author who loved Pugs.

Confucius
For Pekingese or Chow Chows, after the famous Chinese philosopher.

Cuchulain
For brave Irish Wolfhounds; after the hero known as the 'hound of Culann'.

Darwin
For Beagles, after the Victorian naturalist Charles Darwin who journeyed to South America on a boat called *The Beagle*.

Declan
A traditional Irish name, suitable for Irish Setters.

Dim sum
For Chinese dogs such as Pekingese, after the Chinese dumplings traditionally served for lunch.

Douglas
A fine Scots name, suitable for Scottish Terriers.

Droopy
A classic name for Bloodhounds.

Dylan
A classic Welsh male name; for Welsh Terriers.

Edith
For French breeds, such as Poodles; after singer Edith Piaf.

Edwin
For Newfoundland, inspired by Sir Edwin Landseer, the painter after whom the Landseer (the earliest Newfoundland) was named.

Entei
A Pokemon-inspired name for Shiba Inu dogs, after the legendary dog of fire.

Fifi
A fun name for female Poodles.

Finn
A classic name for Irish Wolfhounds.

Fly
A traditional name for Sheepdogs.

Frankfurter
A humorous name for Dachshunds.

Frida
For characterful female Chihuahuas, after Mexican artist Frida Kahlo.

Fred
A laconic name for Bassett Hounds, after the British cartoon strip.

Gazelle
For graceful, fast-running breeds such as Whippets or Greyhounds.

Ginseng
For Chow Chows; inspired by traditional Chinese medicine.

Glen
A traditional name for male Sheepdogs.

Hamlet
For Great Danes, after
Shakespeare's Prince of Denmark.

Hansel
A traditional German name;
for female Dachshunds
or German Shepherds.

Herman
For male German Shepherds.

Ice
For thick-coated dogs such as
Siberian Huskies or St Bernards.

Ivan
A classic Russian male name,
for Borzoi Hounds.

Ivor
A classic male Welsh name, for
Welsh Terriers.

Jen
A popular name for female
Sheepdogs.

Jess
A traditional female Sheepdog
name.

Jock
A classic name for Scottish
Terriers.

Kaiser
A German name for German
breeds such as Dachshunds or
German Shepherds.

Grainne
A traditional Celtic female
name; suitable for Irish
Wolfhounds or Irish Setters.

Gryff
A classic name for Griffons.

Gwen
A classic name for female Collies.

Hamish
For Scottish Terriers.

Katmandhu
A Tibet-inspired name for
Shih Tzu dogs.

Leprechaun
For Irish dogs such as
Wolfhounds or Setters; after
the traditional name given to
the 'Little People'.

Lionheart
For Rhodesian Ridgebacks;
originally used for hunting lions.

Lotte
A classic German female name,
for Dobermanns or Schnauzers.

Lotus
A flower-inspired name for
lovely females, such as Pekingese
or Shiba Inus.

Luath
For Labradors; after the gentle
Labrador in Sheila Burnford's
The Incredible Journey.

Mac
A classic Scots name, ideal for
Highland Terriers.

Macbeth
A Shakespeare-inspired name
for vocal Scottish Terriers who
'murder sleep'.

Mackenzie
A classic male Scottish name,
suitable for Scotties.

Maclaren
A Formula 1 name for fast-
running dogs such as
Greyhounds or Whippets.

Magnus
A classic name for Scottish Terriers.

Meg
A popular female Sheepdog name.

Mequssuk
For Alaskan Malamutes; from
Alaskan for 'shaggy dog'.

Mishkin
A masculine Russian name for
Russian breeds such as Borzois.

Missus
For Dalmatians, after the canine
heroine of Dodic Smith's classic
book *101 Dalmatians*.

Momo
From the Japanese for 'peach',
suitable for soft-furred Japanese
dog breeds.

Moscow
A Russian-inspired name for
Borzoi dogs.

Mungo
A classic Scots name, ideal for
Scottish Terriers.

Niamh
For beautiful Irish Setters; after
an Irish goddess.

Nike
A sportswear-inspired name for
speedy dogs such as Whippets or
Greyhounds.

Nikita
A feminine Russian name for
Russian breeds such as Borzois.

Olivier
For handsome English Hounds,
after acclaimed actor Laurence
Olivier.

Orla
A Celtic name for queenly
female Irish Setters.

Oscar
A Hollywood-inspired name for
prize-winning male dogs.

Otto
A classic German name,
suitable for Dachshunds or
Weimaraners.

Owen
A traditional male Welsh name, suitable for Welsh Border Collies.

Paris
A French-inspired name for Poodles of either sex.

Peking
A classic name for Pekingese dogs of either sex.

Pep
A traditional Welsh name for Sheepdogs.

Pepys
For King Charles Spaniels; after Samuel Pepys who famously kept a diary during Charles's reign.

Pongo
For Dalmatians; after the canine hero of Dodie Smith's classic book *101 Dalmatians*.

Pug
The simple name given to the artist Hogarth's Pug.

Qannik
For Alaskan Malamutes, from the Alaskan for 'snowflake'.

Red
A classic name for Red Setters.

Rhiannan
From the Welsh for 'goddess'; for Welsh Border Collies.

Rocky
For boxers, inspired by the film starring Sylvester Stallone as a gutsy fighter.

Saffron
A spice-inspired name for Red Setters.

Sauerkraut
For German dogs such as Dachshunds.

Schnitzel
A popular name for little Dachshunds.

Scottie
For Scottish Terriers.

Shep
A classic name for male Sheepdogs.

Siegfried
A heroic name for German Shepherds.

Simba
For Rhodesian Ridgebacks, used to hunt lions; from the Swahili for 'lion.'

Speedy
For fast-moving dogs such as Greyhounds.

Swift
For fast-moving dogs such as Greyhounds.

Tao
For philosophical breeds, such as Tosas or Chows.

Tara
For female Irish Setters.

Terry
For Cairn Terriers, after the dog that played Toto the Dog in the classic film *The Wizard of Oz*.

Tess
For female Sheepdogs.

Tiny
A classic, tongue-in-cheek name for Great Danes or Irish Wolfhounds.

Titian
For Red Setters; inspired by the Italian artist obsessed by red-haired models.

Tolstoy
A literary name for Russian breeds, such as Salukis; after the famous Russian playwright.

Tsar
An imperial name for Russian dogs such as Borzois or Salukis.

Tup
For male Sheepdogs.

Tyson
For Boxer dogs; after tough boxing champion Mike Tyson.

Vodka
A drinks-inspired name for Russian dogs of either sex.

Waldmann
For Dachshunds, after Queen Victoria's pet Dachshund.

Wee Jock
A classic Scots name, ideal for small Scottish terriers.

Winston
For bulldogs; after British Prime Minister Winston Churchill.

Winter
For cold-weather breeds such as Huskies or Newfoundlands.

Wolf
A classic name for Wolfhounds.

Wolfgang
A classic name for German breeds such as Weimaraners or Dachshunds.

Yeti
For Shih Tzu dogs, after the infamous Abominable Snowman.

Yorkie
A classic name for Yorkshire Terriers.

Yukon
For sledge dogs such as Malamutes or Huskies.

famous dogs

Argus
Odysseus's loyal dog, who recognised him upon his return to Ithaca.

Barkley
Big Bird's large, lovable dog from popular children's TV series *Sesame Street*.

Barney
President George W. Bush's Scottish Terrier, who lives at the White House.

Beauty
A brave Wirehaired Terrier who searched for survivors in London's rubble after bombing raids during World War II.

Beethoven
The large, friendly canine from the film *Beethoven*.

Bimbo
The name given to Betty Boop's canine friend.

Blaze
President Franklin Delano Roosevelt's Mastiff.

Bruno
Cinderella's lazy, but loyal dog in the Disney classic.

Buddy
President Clinton's chocolate-brown Labrador, named after Clinton's uncle.

Bullseye
Bill Sykes's dog from Charles Dickens' classic novel *Oliver Twist*.

Cafall
King Arthur's loyal dog in Arthurian legend.

Cerberus
The three-headed dog who guarded the kingdom of the dead in Greek mythology.

Crab
The only dog to appear in a Shakespeare play, Crab appears in *Two Gentlemen of Verona*.

Deputy Dawg
The drawling cartoon canine.

Digby
A film-star canine, the biggest dog in the world.

Dill the Dog
The small, excitable dog from children's TV series *The Herbs*.

Dizzy
The Pug belonging to the Duke and Duchess of Windsor.

Dogmatix
The small intrepid dog from Goscinny and Uderzo's *Asterix* comic books.

Dookie
The name of the Corgi given by King George VI to his beloved daughters.

Dougal
The delightfully petulant canine from cult TV children's series *The Magic Roundabout*.

Eddie
The small yet dominating dog from the popular TV sitcom *Frasier*.

Fala
President F. D. Roosevelt's Scottish Terrier, his constant companion.

Fluffy
The three-headed dog that guarded the Philosopher's Stone at Hogwarts School, in J.K. Rowling's best-selling book *Harry Potter and the Philosopher's Stone*.

Flush
After Elizabeth Barrett Browning's beloved Spaniel.

Fussie
The name given to the actress Ellen Terry's Foxhound.

Gelert
A legendary loyal Welsh Wolfhound who killed a wolf that was threatening his master's baby son.

Gnasher
Cheerful cheeky dog, Dennis the Menace's loyal sidekick from the *Beano* comic.

Greyfriars Bobby
The loyal Skye Terrier who stayed guarding his master's grave for fourteen years after his death in 1858. Commemorated to this day by a memorial in Edinburgh.

Gromit
The silent, yet expressive dog who accompanies his owner Wallace in his adventures. Star of Nick Park's animated Wallace and Gromit films.

Hachiko
A loyal Japanese Akita who continued to visit the station his master had returned home to for nine years after his master's death.

Hong Kong Phooey
The crime-fighting hound from the eponymous TV cartoon series *Hong Kong Phooey*.

Jip
Dr Doolittle's loyal dog, from Hugh Lofting's Dr Doolittle books.

Jumble
William Brown's beloved canine companion, from Richmal Crompton's classic children's stories.

Laika
The first living creature to enter orbit, Laika the dog was sent into space by the Russians in 1952.

Lassie
The beautiful, loyal Collie from the classic story by Eric Knight, immortalised in film and TV.

Manchu
Alice Roosevelt's small, black Pekingese, given to her by the Empress of China.

Millie
First Lady Barbara Bush's Springer Spaniel.

Montmorency
The companionable canine from Jerome K. Jerome's comic classic *Three Men in a Boat*.

Nana
The loving, maternal dog from Peter Pan.

Nipper
The Terrier immortalised in the picture 'His Master's Voice', listening attentively to a gramophone.

Noble
The name given to Queen Victoria's Border Collie.

Patsy Ann
A remarkable Bull Terrier appointed official greeter of arriving ships at the Alaskan capital of Juneau.

Pete
President Theodore Roosevelt's Pitbull Terrier.

Petra
The name given to one of the *Blue Peter* dogs.

Rin Tin Tin
The athletic German Shepherd who starred in twenty-six hugely popular films before his death in 1932.

Roobarb
The characterful dog, forever trying to outdo Custard the Cat, from the children's TV cartoon series *Roobarb and Custard*.

Scooby Doo
The greedy, cowardly cartoon star of the eponymous TV series.

Shannon
President John F. Kennedy's Irish Cocker Spaniel.

Sharp
The name given to Queen Victoria's Collie.

Snoopy
The philosophical canine from the popular *Peanuts* cartoons.

Snowy
Tintin's loyal canine companion from Hergé's cult comic books.

Spark
The name given to one of Queen Elizabeth II's Corgi dogs.

Sweep
Sooty's friend, beloved by a whole generation of children.

Taster
President George Washington's hound.

Thisbe
The Spaniel kept by Queen Marie-Antoinette of France.

Toby
A historic name, after the dog in Punch and Judy shows.

Toto
Dorothy's beloved dog from *The Wizard of Oz*.

Tramp
The cheeky mongrel who wins Lady's heart in Disney's classic film *The Lady and the Tramp*.

Wat
The name given to Queen Victoria's Fox Terrier.

White Fang
The tough dog, eponymous hero of Jack London's novel.

Yuki
President Lyndon B. Johnson's cheeky mongrel dog.

famous dogs

girl dogs

Aqua
For water-loving females.

Athena
For wise females, after the stately Greek goddess.

Audrey
A Hollywood-inspired name for elegant females; after actress Audrey Hepburn.

Babe
An endearing name for lovable females.

Baby
An affectionate name for childlike females.

Beauty
A classic name for attractive dogs.

Bella
For lovely dogs, from the Italian for 'beautiful'.

Belle
For lovely dogs, from the French for 'beautiful'.

Bess
A diminutive of Elizabeth.

Betty
An old-fashioned female name.

Blossom
A dainty name for pretty dogs.

Bonnie
An old-fashioned name for cheerful dogs.

Buffy
For intrepid, beautiful females; after *Buffy the Vampire Slayer*.

Candy
For sweet-natured female dogs.

Celia
A traditional female name.

Charlotte
For petite, feminine dogs.

Chelsea
For fashionable dogs.

Cherry
A fruit-inspired name, especially appropriate for red-coated dogs.

Circe
For bewitching females; after the enchantress in Homer's *Odyssey*.

Cleo
For beautiful females, after the Egyptian queen Cleopatra.

Clover
A flower-inspired name for sweet female dogs.

Daisy
A floral name for pretty, dainty dogs.

Darling
An affectionate name for beloved dogs.

Delia
For food-loving dogs; after food writer Delia Smith.

Delilah
A biblical name for courageous female dogs.

Di
A diminutive of Diana, made famous by Princess Diana, or Princess Di as she was affectionately known.

Diana
For hunting females; after the Roman goddess of the hunt.

Dixie
A music-inspired name for female dogs.

Dolly
For small, attractive dogs.

Dorothy
For brave, friendly females; after Dorothy in *The Wizard of Oz*.

Dot
A monosyllabic name, especially suitable for small dogs.

Duchess
For aristocratic females.

Emma
An old-fashioned female name.

Felicity
For happy girl dogs.

Fleur
From the French for 'flower', for pretty females.

Flirt
For engaging females.

Flora
For flower-loving females; from the Latin for 'flower'.

Flossie
An old-fashioned popular female name.

Fluffy
For long-haired female dogs.

Francine
A popular female name.

Freya
After the Norse goddess.

Frieda
For peaceful, happy dogs.

Frou-Frou
A French-inspired name for dainty females.

Funny Girl
An affectionate name for a much-loved pet.

Gaia
For down-to-earth females, after the earth goddess.

Garbo
For beautiful, solitary dogs; after the silent movie star Greta Garbo.

Gem
A simple name for treasured females.

Gemma
For precious females, from the Italian for 'gem'.

Gert
Short for Gertrude, an old-fashioned name.

Gigi
A French-inspired name for pretty dogs.

Girl
A simple but popular name for female dogs.

Grace
For graceful females.

Gretel
A traditional German name, suitable for female Dachshunds or German Shepherds.

Guinevere
For queenly females.

Helen
For lovely dogs, after legendary beauty Helen of Troy.

Hermione
For clever, brave females, after Harry Potter's friend in J.K. Rowlings's children's books.

Holly
A plant-inspired name for sharp-clawed females.

Jackie
For elegant females, after Jackie Kennedy.

Jade
For attractive females, after the semi-precious stone.

Jane
For clever ladylike dogs, after the writer Jane Austen.

Jasmine
A flower-inspired name.

Jazz
A music-inspired name for rhythmic females.

Jeannie
An old-fashioned name.

Jemima
A homely, feminine name.

Jessie
For graceful female dogs.

Jewel
For precious female pets.

Jill
A popular female name.

Jo
For strong-willed females; after the heroine of the book *Little Women*.

Joan
For intrepid females; after French patriot Joan of Arc.

Josephine
An old-fashioned female name.

Judy
A simple, classic female dog name.

Juliet
For romantic females, after the Shakespearian heroine.

Kay
A monosyllabic name.

Kiki
A pretty, French name for female dogs.

Kylie
For blonde females, after Australian pop star Kylie Minogue.

Lady
For well-mannered females.

Lara
A romantic name for beautiful females.

Lass
A Scottish term for females.

Layla
An Eric Clapton-inspired name for female dogs.

Leah
A biblical name, meaning 'languid'.

Lily
A flower-inspired name for female dogs.

Lola
A lovely female name.

Lucy
A classic name for bright dogs.

Luna
For moon-loving females, from the Latin for 'moon'.

Madame
For well-behaved females.

Madeleine
A feminine, French name.

Madonna
For charismatic females; after the famous singer.

Mama
For motherly females.

Mango
A fruit-inspired name for sweet-natured, females.

Marigold
A flower-inspired name for golden females.

Marina
For water-loving females.

Marlene
For elegant slender females; after screen goddess Marlene Dietrich.

Mata Hari
For seductive females; after the famous spy.

Meg
A monosyllabic female name.

Megan
A popular female name for collies.

Mia
For possessive females; from the Italian for 'mine'.

Mignon
From the French for 'sweet'.

Millicent
An old-fashioned female name.

Mimi
A pretty, feminine name.

Mimosa
A flower-inspired name, especially suitable for fluffy-furred dogs.

Minnie
For small females; after cartoon character Minnie Mouse.

Miss Moneypenny
For well-behaved females, after the secretary in the James Bond films.

Mo
A monosyllabic name.

Molly
A popular female name.

Morgan
For entrancing females; after sorceress Morgan le Fay.

Nancy
An old-fashioned female name.

Nirvana
For blissful dogs.

Opal
A jewel-inspired name for precious dogs.

Pandora
For glamorous females; after the figure in Greek mythology whose name meant 'all gifts'.

Peaches
A fruit-inspired name for lovely dogs.

Peggy
For seductive females; after singer Peggy Lee.

Perdita
Meaning 'lost', so especially appropriate for rescue dogs.

Phoebe
From the Greek word meaning 'bright'.

Poppet
An affectionate name for endearing dogs.

Poppy
A flower-inspired name for pretty dogs.

Primrose
For dainty female dogs; after the pale yellow flower.

Princess
For regal female dogs with demanding ways.

Queenie
A classic name for regal females.

Rita
For beautiful females; after Hollywood star Rita Hayworth.

Rosemary
A herb-inspired name for female dogs.

Rosie
A floral name for pretty female canines.

Roxy
A showbiz name for female dogs.

Ruby
A gem-inspired name for precious female dogs.

Samantha
A classic girl's name.

Scarlett
Fo strong-willed, attractive females, after Scarlett O'Hara of *Gone with the Wind*.

Scrumptious
For delicious female dogs.

Stella
For night-loving females; from the Latin for 'star'.

Sugar
For sweet-natured female dogs.

Suzi
A classic girl's name.

Tara
An aristocratic name for elegant female dogs.

Tasha
A popular female name.

Tiffany
For sparkly-eyed females; after the world-famous jewellery store.

Tina
For energetic females; after rock star Tina Turner.

Tootsie
A humorous name for females.

Trixie
An endearing name for female canines.

Venice
For water-loving dogs; after the romantic Italian city of canals.

Victoria
For well-behaved regal females; after Queen Victoria.

Violet
A flower-inspired name for small, shy females; inspired by the phrase 'shrinking violet'.

Zenobia
For regal females, after an Egyptian queen.

Zoe
An elegant female name.

Zuleika
For dazzling females; from the Persian for 'brilliant beauty'.

girl dogs

boy dogs

Adonis
For handsome male dogs, after the figure in Greek mythology.

Albert
A traditional name, inspired by Queen Victoria's beloved husband Prince Albert.

Alfie
A down-to-earth name for cheeky dogs.

Algernon
An old-fashioned name.

Algie
An affectionate masculine name.

Anubis
After the jackal-headed god of Ancient Egyptian mythology.

Apollo
For sunny-natured dogs, after the Greek god of the sun.

Aragorn
A *The Lord of the Rings*-inspired name for brave, heroic dogs.

Archibald
An impressive, traditional name.

Arthur
For noble males, after King Arthur.

Aristotle
For thoughtful males, after the famous philosopher.

Arnold
An old-fashioned name for male dogs.

Bart
A humorous name, inspired by cult animation *The Simpsons*.

Basil
A herb-inspired name for dogs.

Beau
For handsome male dogs.

Beau Brummell
For elegant dogs, after the dapper eighteenth-century dandy.

Benji
A popular name, a diminutive of Benjamin.

Bentley
A classy name for dignified dogs.

Beowulf
For courageous dogs; after the Norse hero.

Bernard
An old-fashioned, dignified dog's name.

Bert
A cheery, monosyllabic name.

Bertie
For dim-witted but sweet-natured dogs, after Wodehouse's comic creation Bertie Wooster.

Bilbo
A Tolkien-inspired name for small, friendly dogs; after Bilbo Baggins the hobbit.

Bilko
For comfort-seeking hounds, after Sergeant Bilko on the comic Phil Silvers' show.

Bob
A simple, down-to-earth name.

Bongo
A rhythmic name for music-loving dogs.

Boomer
For deep-voiced male dogs.

Boss
For impressive, commanding canine that rule the house.

Boy
A classic name for male dogs.

Brendan
A traditional Celtic male name, derived from the word 'prince'.

Brian
A down-to-earth name for male dogs.

Bruce
A classic Scots name; after Scottish hero Robert the Bruce.

Byron
A literary name for dashing dogs; after the English Romantic poet Lord Byron.

Calloway
For vocal males; after jazz singer Cab Calloway.

Casanova
For amorous males; after the famous Latin lover.

Chaplin
For comic male dogs; after film star Charlie Chaplin.

Charlie
A down-to-earth male name.

Chester
A dignified, old-fashioned name.

Clint
For tough, macho dogs; after film star Clint Eastwood.

Courteney
A stylish name for boy dogs.

Dandy
For elegant male dogs.

Danny
A down-to-earth name, short for Daniel.

Dante
A literary name for male dogs, after the famous medieval Italian poet.

Dean
A Hollywood-inspired name for handsome dogs; after film star James Dean.

Deputy
For loyal, obedient dogs.

Dexter
For cool dogs; after the jazz musician Dexter Gordon.

Don Juan
For handsome, serial romancers; after the famous Latin lover.

Donatello
An artistic name for male dogs; after the renowned Renaissance artist.

Dracula
For night-loving dogs; after the Transylvanian vampire.

Dylan
For handsome male dogs; after singer Bob Dylan.

Fairbanks
For dashing dogs; after Hollywood film star Douglas Fairbanks.

Ferguson
A grand name for strong male dogs.

Finnigan
A traditional Irish name.

Fitzpatrick
An old-fashioned name.

Fletcher
A simple name for male dogs.

Flintoff
For large, sporting dogs, after the English cricketer, Andrew Flintoff.

Frankenstein
A horror movie-inspired name for male dogs.

Freeway
A road-inspired name or fast-moving dogs.

Frodo
For small but intrepid dogs, after the hobbit hero in *The Lord of the Rings*.

Galahad
For noble dogs; after the knight of the Round Table.

Gameboy
A game-inspired name for playful dogs.

Gandhi
For charismatic but peaceful dogs; after Mahatma Gandhi.

Ganesh
For genial dogs, after the Hindu elephant god.

Garibaldi
For independent dogs; after the Italian patriot (or the biscuit!).

Garrison
A classic American name.

Geoffrey
An old-fashioned name for boy dogs.

George
A down-to-earth, simple name.

Geronimo
For warrior dogs, after the Apache chief.

Gilbert
For faithful, trusted dogs.

Gimli
A *The Lord of the Rings*-inspired

name for loyal, fighting dogs; after Gimli the dwarf.

Godzilla
For large terrifying male dogs; after the Japanese monster.

Goliath
For large dogs; after the biblical warrior.

Gomez
A masculine Mexican name.

Gonzo
A humorous name for male canines.

Gus
An affectionate, diminutive form of Angus.

Guy
A monosyllabic name for male dogs.

boy dogs

Hadrian
For imperial dogs; after the Roman emperor.

Harris
A down-to-earth name for dogs.

Harry
A classic name for male dogs.

Hector
For heroic dogs; after the hero of Greek mythology.

Henry
A traditional masculine name.

Hercules
For strong dogs; after the legendary hero of Greek mythology.

Homer
A literary name for intelligent dogs; after the Greek poet.

Horatio
For sea-loving dogs; after British Admiral Horatio Nelson.

Houdini
For dogs good at getting out of a tight spot; after the famous escapologist.

Igor
For large, loyal dogs; after the horror movie manservant.

Ivanhoe
For brave dogs; after the hero of Walter Scott's novel.

Jackie
For lively dogs who enjoy a good fight; after martial arts hero Jackie Chan.

Jack
A popular classic dog name.

Jake
For simple dogs.

Jeff
A down-to-earth monosyllabic name for peaceful dogs.

Jerome
An old-fashioned masculine name.

Jimmy
For rebellious dogs; after film star James Dean.

Joe
A neat, straightforward name.

Joseph
Meaning 'an addition to the family'.

Jove
For regal dogs; after the mythological figure.

Jupiter
For regal dogs; after the Roman king of the gods.

Karloff
For large monstrous dogs; after actor Boris Karloff, star of numerous horror movies.

Kennedy
For handsome charismatic dogs; after President John F. Kennedy.

King Kong
For formidable, large male dogs.

Krishna
For charismatic dogs; after the Hindu god.

Laddie
A Scottish name for male dogs.

Lancelot
For handsome, gallant dogs, after the knight of the Round Table.

Legolas
For fearless, graceful dogs; after the elf hero of *The Lord of the Rings*.

Lennon
For intellectual males; after Beatle John Lennon.

Lennox
For tough dogs, after boxer Lennox Lewis.

Lopez
A masculine Mexican name.

Lucifer
For handsome yet devilish dogs.

Ludwig
An old-fashioned, Germanic name for victorious dogs.

Luke
A *Star Wars*-inspired name for intrepid dogs; after Luke Skywalker.

Macaulay
An historical name for male dogs.

Mandela
For dignified dogs; after Nelson Mandela.

Mario
A classic Italian male name.

Marley
For laid-back males; after Bob Marley.

Marlowe
For shrewd, observant dogs; after Raymond Chandler's literary private eye.

Mars
For warlike dogs, after the Roman god of war.

Marshall
For loyal deputy dogs.

Max
A simple, classic dog name.

Maxwell
An old-fashioned masculine name.

Mercury
For fast-moving males; after the Greek god who, with his winged sandals, was the messenger of the gods.

Merlin
For wizardly dogs; after the wizard of Arthurian myth.

Michelangelo
An artistic name for dogs, inspired by the Renaissance artist.

Micro
A contemporary name for small dogs.

Middleton
A distinguished, formal name.

Midget
A classic name for small dogs.

Milo
A simple boy's name, derived from the names Miles.

Mishka
A Russian name for big, bear-like dogs.

Moose
A humorous, animal-inspired name for large dogs.

Morris
A traditional name for boy dogs.

Mortimer
An old-fashioned male name.

Mozart
A musical name for male dogs.

Nehru
For handsome, charismatic male dogs; after the Indian Prime Minister.

Nelson
For courageous, water-loving dogs; after British sea hero Admiral Horatio Nelson.

Noël
From the French for 'Christmas'. Especially appropriate for a puppy received as a Christmas present.

boy dogs

Orion
For hunting hounds; after the legendary hunter.

Orson
For charismatic, clever dogs; after legendary director Orson Welles.

Perseus
For heroic dogs; after the hero of Greek mythology.

Plato
For intelligent dogs; after the famous Greek philosopher.

Raleigh
For brave, exploring dogs; after Sir Walter Raleigh.

Ralph
An old-fashioned, elegant name for dapper dogs.

Rambo
For tough, macho male dogs.

Raphael
For handsome males; after the Renaissance artist.

Rembrandt
For talented male dogs after the Dutch artist.

Rex
A traditional name from the Latin for 'king', so especially apt for regal dogs.

Rhett
For handsome male dogs with an eye for the ladies; after the charming Rhett Butler in *Gone With the Wind*.

Riley
For lucky dogs who live the proverbial 'life of Riley'.

Robin
For dogs who enjoy breaking the law; after outlaw Robin Hood.

Rolf
A name derived from the Old Norse for 'wolf'.

Romeo
A Shakespearian name for romantic male dogs.

Rollo
A traditional name, especially appropriate for macho dogs.

Rufus
A classic dog's name.

Sailor Boy
For dogs with a taste for life on the ocean wave.

Sam
A classic dog name, very popular in America.

Shakespeare
A literary name for male dogs; after the Bard.

Shane
For tough but noble dogs; after the classic American cowboy hero.

Sheriff
For obedient, law-abiding dogs, inspired by American Westerns.

Sherlock
For intelligent dogs; after the great detective Sherlock Holmes.

Shogun
For courageous, macho dogs; after the historic Japanese commander-in-chief.

Shrek
For large, gentle dogs, after the cartoon character.

Sigmund
For intellectual dogs; after the father of psychotherapy, Sigmund Freud.

Sinbad
For adventurous dogs; after Sinbad the sailor.

Sir
An old-fashioned, respectful name for male dogs.

Solomon
For wise dogs; after King Solomon.

Sophocles
For thoughtful dogs; after the Greek philosopher.

Spartacus
For brave, independent dogs;
after the Roman slave.

Tarquin
An old Roman name, for
noble males.

Templeton
An old-fashioned name for dogs.

Tiny Tim
For small (or large) dogs after
the young boy in Dickens'
A Christmas Carol.

Tobermory
A traditional name for male dogs.

Toggle
A homely name for dogs who are
attached to their owners.

Tolstoy
A literary name for noble
male dogs; after the famous
Russian author.

Tristan
For gallant male dogs; after
the knight of Arthurian legend.

Valentino
For romantic dogs, after matinee
idol Rudolph Valentino.

Voltaire
For thoughtful, intelligent dogs;
after the famous French writer
and philosopher.

Walt
For humorous dogs; after
animator Walt Disney.

Watson
For loyal dogs; after Doctor
Watson, Sherlock Holmes's
faithful sidekick.

Wayne
For tough dogs; after actor
John Wayne, noted for his
portrayal of cowboys.

Wilbur
An down-to-earth male name.

Woody
For neurotic dogs; after film
director Woody Allen.

Zack
A monosyllabic male name.

Zeus
For charismatic, dominating
males; after the Greek god.

Zorro
For dashing dogs, after the
literary hero.

colourful dogs

Amber
For golden-coloured females.

Ash
For silver-grey canines of
either sex.

Barley
For golden-furred dogs of
either sex.

Bianca
For white female dogs; from the
Italian for 'white'. Bianco is
the masculine version.

Blackberry
A fruit-inspired name for black
dogs of either sex.

Blackie
A classic name for black dogs.

Blanc
For white dogs; from the French
for 'white'.

Blanco
For white dogs; from the
Spanish for 'white'.

Blondie
For golden-haired female dogs.

Boots
For dogs with distinctive
markings on their paws.

Bran
For black dogs; from the Old
Irish for 'raven'.

Brownie
A food-inspired name for
chocolate-brown dogs of
either sex.

Bruno
For brown male dogs.

Butterscotch
A sweet-inspired name for
golden dogs of either sex.

Cadbury
For chocolate-brown male dogs.

Cappuccino
For coffee-coloured dogs
of either sex.

Caramel
For golden-coloured dogs
of either sex.

Carbon
For black dogs of either sex.

Carob
For chocolate-coloured dogs
of either sex.

Casper
For white male dogs; after the
famous cartoon ghost.

Charcoal
For black or dark grey dogs of
either sex.

Chestnut
A nut-inspired name for brown
dogs of either sex.

Chocolate
For chocolate-brown dogs
of either sex.

Cider
A drink-inspired name for golden dogs of either sex.

Cinnamon
A spice-inspired name for brown dogs of either sex.

Cloud
For white or light-grey dogs of either sex.

Cocoa
For chocolate-brown dogs of either sex.

Cookie
A biscuit-inspired name for brown dogs of either sex.

Copper
A metal-inspired name for golden-red dogs of either sex.

Custard
A food-inspired name for golden dogs of either sex.

Darth
A *Star Wars*-inspired name for black, male dogs.

Dotty
For spotty female dogs.

Dusty
A popular name for silver-grey dogs of either sex.

Espresso
For fast and energetic, coffee-coloured male dogs.

Fay
For beautiful blond canines; after archetypal blonde Fay Wray, star of the classic film *King Kong*.

Foxy
A popular name for red-brown dogs of either sex.

Freckles
For spotted dogs of either sex.

Frosty
For white-coated dogs.

Gandalf
A *The Lord of the Rings*-inspired name for grey male dogs, after the wizard Gandalf the Grey.

Ginger Snap
For ginger-coated dogs of either sex.

Gold
A precious-metal-inspired name for golden-furred canines of either sex.

Goldie
For golden-furred canines of either sex.

Goldilocks
For golden-furred female dogs.

Guinness
For dark-brown and cream canines, after the famous Irish stout.

Hazel
A nut-inspired name for brown dogs of either sex.

Honey
A popular name for golden-furred female dogs.

Inkspots
For spotted dogs of either sex.

Inky
A name for black dogs of either sex.

Iris
For multi-coloured females; after the Roman goddess of the rainbow.

Java
For coffee-coloured dogs of either sex; after the Indonesian island noted for its coffee.

Jet
For jet-black canines of either sex.

Ladybird
For spotted female dogs.

Latte
For white dogs of either sex; from the Italian for 'milk'.

Leo
A classic name for golden-coated dogs; from the Latin for 'lion'.

Macaroon
For biscuit-coloured dogs of either sex.

Magnolia
A flower-inspired name for cream-coloured female dogs.

Marilyn
For lovely, golden-haired females; after iconic blonde Marilyn Monroe.

Mars
For chocolate-coloured dogs.

Midnight
For black-coated dogs.

Milou
For white dogs; from the French name for Snowy, Tintin's faithful dog.

Mint
A sweet-inspired name for white dogs of either sex.

Moby
For large white male dogs; after the Great White Whale in Melville's novel *Moby Dick*.

Mocha
For coffee-coloured dogs of either sex.

Molasses
For sweet-tempered, dark-brown dogs of either sex.

Moonbeam
For white dogs of either sex.

Moonshadow
A poetic name for grey male dogs.

Mouse
For small, soft-grey dogs of either sex.

Mustard
For mustard-brown dogs of either sex.

Nero
For black dogs; from the Italian for 'black'.

Othello
A Shakespeare-inspired name for handsome black male dogs.

Panda
For black-and-white dogs.

Patch
A popular name for dogs, especially those with a patch over one eye.

Pearl
For beautiful, white female dogs.

colourful dogs

49

Peppermint
A sweet-inspired name for white dogs of either sex.

Phantom
For grey-white dogs.

Phoenix
For golden dogs of either sex; after the mythical golden bird.

Puffin
An affectionate bird-inspired name for black-and-white dogs.

Raccoon
An animal-inspired name for black-and-white dogs.

Rainbow
For multi-coloured dogs.

Raven
A bird-inspired name for black dogs of either sex.

Redwood
A tree-inspired name for red-coated dogs.

Rum
For golden-brown dogs of either sex; after the drink.

Rusty
For golden-brown dogs.

Sandy
For golden dogs of either sex.

Silver
An elegant name for silver-grey dogs of either sex.

Simba
For golden-brown dogs, after Disney's *The Lion King*.

Snowball
For white dogs of either sex.

Sooty
A classic name for black dogs of either sex.

Spot
A simple name for spotted dogs of either sex.

Spotty
For spotted dogs of either sex.

Toffee
For golden-brown dogs.

Vader
A *Star Wars*-inspired name for formidable, black male dogs.

Vanilla
For cream-coloured, female dogs.

Wellington
For dogs with distinctive markings on their paws.

Whisky
A drink-inspired name for golden-brown dogs.

colourful dogs

characterful dogs

Adamnan
For shy male dogs; from the Celtic for 'timid one'.

Admiral
For water-loving male dogs.

Alma
For well-behaved females; from the Celtic for 'good'.

Amica
For amicable female dogs; from the Italian for 'friend'.

Amigo
For friendly male dogs; from the Spanish for 'friend'.

Aquarius
A horoscope-inspired name for water-loving dogs of either sex.

Baci
For affectionate dogs, from the Italian for 'kisses'.

Bamboozle
For clever canines that are very good at deceiving their owners.

Banshee
For vocal dogs of either sex.

Barnacle
For dogs who like to stick closely to their owners.

Bashful
For shy dogs.

Bonbon
For sweet female dogs; from the French for 'sweet'.

Boomer
For big-voiced male dogs.

Bosun
For loyal, seafaring dogs.

Brendan
For exploring dogs; after the Irish saint.

Bubbles
For cheerful, rather dim females.

Buddha
For calm male dogs.

Caesar
For commanding dogs; after Roman emperor Julius Caesar.

Cagney
For tough dogs; after Hollywood actor James Cagney, noted for his portrayal of gangsters.

Champ
For champion male dogs.

Chaplin
For humorous male dogs; after silent movie star Charlie Chaplin.

Chaser
For dogs who enjoy chasing.

Cheddar
A food-inspired name; after the famous British cheese.

Cherub
For affectionate, male dogs.

Chewy
A self-explanatory name for dogs of either sex.

Chief
For male dogs who rule the roost.

Chilli
For hot-tempered dogs.

Ciao
For friendly dogs; from the Italian for 'hello'.

Columbus
For male dogs who like exploring.

Cuddles
For affectionate dogs of either sex.

Daredevil
For intrepid dogs with a sense of adventure.

Dino
A classic male name.

Dizzy
For rush-around dogs of either sex.

Dozy
For sleep-loving canines of either sex.

Dracula
For dogs with a tendency to bite.

Duke
A classic name for grand, noble male dogs.

Dynamite
An explosive name for destructive hounds.

Dynamo
For energetic male dogs.

Earl
For noble dogs.

Faithful
An affectionate name for loyal male dogs.

Fearless
For brave boy dogs.

Felix
For happy male dogs; from the Latin for 'happy'.

Fergus
For energetic males; from the Gaelic for 'man of vigour'.

Fidel
For loyal dogs; from the Latin for 'faithful'.

Flash
For super-speedy dogs.

Flurry
For dogs who are always in a hurry.

Freedom
For independent dogs of either sex.

Frisky
For lively dogs of either sex.

Gallant
For noble male canines.

Genius
For super-intelligent dogs of either sex.

Gobble
For greedy male dogs.

Good Boy
An appreciative name for male dogs.

Good Girl
An appreciative name for female canines.

Gourmet
For dogs who enjoy fine food.

Greedy
An apt name for dogs with a voracious appetite.

Groucho
For grumpy dogs; after wise-cracking film star Groucho Marx.

Grumpy
For bad-tempered male dogs.

Happy
For cheerful dogs of either sex.

Harley
For fast-moving male dogs; after the famous motorbike.

Hope
A traditional name for optimistic females.

Hugo
For thoughtful male dogs; from the Old German for 'thought'.

Imp
For mischievous boy dogs.

Intrepid
For brave male dogs.

Jeopardy
For dogs who like taking chances.

Jolly
For cheerful dogs of either sex.

Joy
For happy female dogs.

Kali
For destructive females; after the Hindu goddess.

Leonardo
For clever male dogs; after the Renaissance genius Leonardo da Vinci.

Liability
For dogs who are a definitely a big responsibility for their owners.

Limpet
For dogs who stick closely to their owners.

Livingstone
For exploring dogs, after Victorian explorer David Livingstone.

Loco
For mad male dogs.

Loopy
Cheerful name for mad dogs of either sex.

Lunatic
An affectionate name for nonsensical dogs.

Macchiavelli
For shrewd operators; after the historic figure, advisor to the Medici family in Renaissance Florence.

Mad
A straightforward name for reckless, playful dogs of either sex.

Mad Max
For rebellious males; after the film starring Mel Gibson.

Maestro
For charismatic male dogs.

Majesty
For regal male dogs.

Major
A military name for dominant male dogs.

Maniac
A self-explanatory name for mad dogs.

Maple
For sweet-natured dogs; after maple syrup.

Marco Polo
For dogs who like exploring; after the famous Italian traveller.

Mate
A simple name for friendly male dogs.

Maverick
For independent-minded dogs.

Mayflower
For pioneering dogs; after the ship that America's early settlers travelled on.

Menace
For dangerous male dogs.

Mischief
For dogs who enjoy getting up to no good.

Moody
For temperamental male dogs.

Morning
For dogs who enjoy rising early.

Morpheus
For dozy dogs; after the Greek god of sleep.

Mustard
For hot-tempered dogs of either sex.

Napoleon
For small, charismatic dogs; after Napoleon Bonaparte.

Naughty
For mischievous, badly-behaved canines of either sex.

Nelson
For water-loving dogs; after the notable British admiral.

Neutron
For small, energetic dogs, inspired by the elementary particle.

Noble
For dignified male dogs.

Old Faithful
For reliable dogs; after the American geyser.

characterful dogs

57

Pal
A classic name for friendly canines of either sex.

Patience
An old-fashioned name for patient females.

Pazzo
For exuberant dogs, from the Italian for 'mad'.

Penelope
For faithful females; after Odysseus's loyal wife in Homer's epic poem *The Odyssey*.

Pharaoh
For regal, commanding dogs, after the kings of ancient Egypt.

Prudence
An old-fashioned name for cautious females.

Ragamuffin
An old-fashioned name for mucky pups.

Rajah
For imperial male dogs, after the term for an Indian king or prince.

Reckless
For dogs who enjoy taking risks.

Rex
For noble male dogs; from the Latin for 'king'.

Risky
For dogs who like to take a chance.

Rogue
For troublesome, naughty male canines.

Rowdy
For noisy, rumbustious dogs.

Royal
For dignified, regal dogs.

Ruffian
For badly-behaved, but endearing male dogs.

Runner
For speedy dogs of either sex.

Samurai
Inspired by the Japanese warrior; for heroic male dogs.

Scamp
An endearing name for cheeky male dogs.

Scoundrel
For male dogs who get up to no good.

Shah
A regal name for male dogs.

Shiva
For powerful male dogs, after the Indian deity.

Skipper
For dogs that like to be in charge.

Sky
For dogs of either sex with a love of wide, open spaces.

Sloth
For sleep-loving male dogs.

Snaggletooth
An expressive name for large-toothed dogs.

Snap
For dogs with a tendency to bite.

Snarl
An expressive name for bad-tempered dogs.

Snuggles
For cuddly dogs of either sex.

Socrates
For male dogs of a thoughtful nature, after the Greek philosopher and teacher.

Solo
For independent dogs who enjoy their own company.

Spumante
A drink-inspired name for bubbly dogs of either sex.

Sparky
For alert, clever male dogs.

Sultan
For regal male dogs.

Sunny
For cheerful dogs of either sex.

Teaser
For dogs with a sense of mischief, that enjoy playing with their owners.

T-bone
A steak-inspired name for greedy male dogs.

Tiara
For elegant female dogs, with something of the princess about them.

Titan
For large aggressive dogs; after the giants of Greek mythology.

Tricky
For dogs you have to keep an eye on.

Trouble
A classic name for dogs who get up to no good.

Tug
For determined dogs, who like to hold on to whatever they have got.

Tutankhamun
For regal dogs, after the ancient Egyptian boy king.

Trusty
For reassuringly reliable dogs.

Wag
For happy dogs of either sex.

Walker
For male dogs who live for their daily walk.

Warrior
For male fighting dogs.

Wasabi
For hot-tempered dogs of either sex; after the Japanese variety of horseradish.

Whirlwind
For wildly energetic dogs of either sex, that leave chaos behind them...

Wild Thing
A rock 'n' roll name for dogs of either sex that walk on the wild side.

Wily
For cunning dogs.

Wonderdog
A self-explanatory name for male or female dogs that are wonderful in every way.

Zebedee
For energetic male dogs; after the bouncing character in *The Magic Roundabout*.

characterful dogs

dog pairs

Batman and Robin
For faithful friends, after the intrepid superheroes.

Bert and Ernie
For bickering duos, from the popular TV show *Sesame Street*.

Castor and Pollux
After the legendary twins, immortalised as a heavenly constellation.

Ebony and Ivory
A piano-inspired pair of names for black and white dogs.

Fred and Ginger
After movie dancers Fred Astaire and Ginger Rogers.

Jekyll and Hyde
For a pair of dogs with very different personalities, after Robert Louis Stevenson's schizophrenic creation.

Kirk and Spock
For a couple of loyal comrades; inspired by *Star Trek*, the cult TV sci-fi series.

Pooh and Piglet
For a lovable pair of hounds, after A.A. Milne's bear of very little brain and his loyal friend.

Port and Starboard
Nautical terms for sea-loving dogs.

Romulus and Remus
After the intrepid twins who founded Rome.

Rough and Tumble
For a pair of energetic dogs who love rolling around.

Rum and Coke
Drink-inspired names for a pair of dark brown dogs.

Salt and Pepper
For white and grey canines of either sex.

Sherlock and Watson
For investigating dogs, after the famous detective Sherlock Holmes and his loyal sidekick Doctor Watson.

Stan and Ollie
For canine jokers, after film comics Stan Laurel and Ollie Hardy.

Tarzan and Jane
After the jungle-dwelling duo.

Tick and Tock
Clockwork names for a pair of punctual dogs.

Topsy and Turvy
For a pair of chaotic dogs.

Tweedledum and Tweedledee
For dogs with totally opposing characters, after Lewis Carroll's twins in *Through the Looking-Glass*.

Wellington and Boots
For dogs with a penchant for chewing shoes; inspired by the waterproof boots.

Yin and Yang
Philosophic names for a pair of thoughtful dogs.

picture credits

Chris Tubbs Pages 2, 4, 7, 8, 9, 14, 15, 16, 17, 18, 19, 20, 25, 29, 30, 31, 32, 34, 35, 36, 37, 38, 39, 42, 43, 48, 49, 61, 62

Chris Everard Pages 5, 11 both, 12, 28, 45 both, 51, 58 both

Andrew Wood Pages 1, 23, 24, 46, 47, 50, 57

Lena Ikse Bergman Pages 26, 27, 33, 40, 41, 59, 60

Christopher Drake Pages 3, 6, 54, 55

Francesca Yorke Endpapers, pages 52, 53

Tom Leighton Pages 22, 56

Jan Baldwin Page 64